The Plant Based Diet Cookbook For Beginners

A Beginners Cookbook with High Protein Meals, Easy and Budget Friendly, the Best Way to Lose Weight Faster.

Valerie Harvey

Table of Contents

written consent from the Publisher. All additional right reserved.The information in the following pages is broadly considered a truthful and accurate account of facts and as such, any inattention, use, or misuse of the information in question by the reader will render any resulting actions solely under their purview. There are no scenarios in which the publisher or the original author of this work can be in any fashion deemed liable for any hardship or damages that may befall them after undertaking information described herein. Additionally, the information in the following pages is intended only for informational purposes and should thus be thought of as universal. As befitting its nature, it is presented without assurance regarding its prolonged validity or interim quality. Trademarks that are mentioned are done without written consent and can in no way be considered an endorsement from the trademark holder.

Introduction

A plant-based diet is a diet based primarily on whole plant foods. It is identical to the regular diet we're used to already, except that it leaves out foods that are not exclusively from plants. Hence, a plant-based diet does away with all types of animal-sourced foods, hydrogenated oils, refined sugars, and processed foods. A whole food plant-based diet comprises not just fruits and vegetables; it also consists of unprocessed or barely-processed oils with healthy monounsaturated fats (like extra-virgin olive oil), whole grains, legumes (essentially lentils and beans), seeds and nuts, as well as herbs and spices. What makes a plant-based meal (or any meal) fun is the manner with which you make them; the seasoning process; and the combination process that contributes to a fantastic flavor and makes every meal unique and enjoyable. There are lots of delicious recipes (all plant-centered), which will prove helpful in when you intend making mouthwatering, healthy plant-based dishes for personal or household consumption. Provided you're eating these plant-based foods regularly, you'll have very problems with fat or diseases that result from bad dietary habits, and there would be no need for excessive calorie tracking. Plant-based diet recipes are versatile; they range from colorful Salads to Lentil Stews, and Bean Burritos. The recipes also draw influences from around the globe, with Mexican, Chinese, European, Indian cuisines all part of the vast array of plant-based recipes available to choose from. Why You Ought to Reduce Your Intake of Processed and Animal-Based Foods. You have likely heard over and over that processed food has adverse effects on your health. You might have also been told repeatedly to stay away from foods with lots of preservatives; nevertheless, nobody ever offered any genuine or concrete facts about why you ought to avoid these foods and why they are unsafe. Consequently, let us properly dissect it to help you properly comprehend why you ought to stay away from these healthy eating offenders. They have massive habit-forming characteristics. Humans have a predisposition towards being addicted to some specific foods; however, the reality is that the fault is not wholly ours. Every one of the unhealthy treats we relish now and then triggers the dopamine release in our brains. This creates a pleasurable effect in our brain, but the excitement is usually short-lived. The discharged dopamine additionally causes an attachment connection gradually, and this is the reason some people consistently go back to eat certain unhealthy foods even when they know it's unhealthy and unnecessary. You can get rid of this by taking out that inducement completely. They are sugar-laden and plenteous in glucose-fructose syrup. Animal-based and processed foods are laden with refined sugars and glucose-fructose syrup which has almost no beneficial food nutrient. An ever-increasing number of studies are affirming what several people presumed from the start; that genetically modified foods bring about inflammatory bowel disease, which consequently makes it increasingly difficult for the body to assimilate essential nutrients. The disadvantages that result from your body being unable to assimilate essential nutrients from consumed foods rightly cannot be overemphasized. Processed and animal-based food products contain plenteous amounts of refined carbohydrates. Indeed, your body requires carbohydrates to give it the needed energy to run body capacities. In any case, refining carbs dispenses with the fundamental supplements; in the way that refining entire grains disposes of the whole grain part. What remains, in the wake of refining, is what's considered as empty carbs or empty calories. These can negatively affect the metabolic system in your body by sharply increasing your blood sugar and insulin quantities. They contain lots of synthetic ingredients. At the point when your body is taking in non-natural ingredients, it regards them as foreign substances. Your body treats them as a health threat. Your body isn't accustomed to identifying synthetic compounds like sucralose or these synthesized sugars. Hence, in defense of your health against this foreign "aggressor," your body does what it's capable of to safeguard your health. It sets off an immune reaction to tackle this "enemy" compound, which indirectly weakens your body's general disease alertness, making you susceptible to illnesses. The concentration and energy expended by your body in ensuring your immune system remain safe could instead be devoted somewhere else. They contain constituent elements that set off an excitable reward sensation in your body. A part of processed and animal-based foods contain compounds like glucose-fructose syrup, monosodium glutamate, and specific food dyes that can trigger some addiction. They rouse your body to receive a benefit in return whenever you consume them. Monosodium glutamate, for example, is added to many store-bought baked foods. This additive slowly conditions your palates to relish the taste. It gets mental just by how your brain interrelates with your taste sensors.

This reward-centric arrangement makes you crave it increasingly, which ends up exposing you to the danger of over consuming calories.

For animal protein, usually, the expression "subpar" is used to allude to plant proteins since they generally have lower levels of essential amino acids as against animal-sourced protein. Nevertheless, what the vast majority don't know is that large amounts of essential amino acids can prove detrimental to your health. Let me break it down further for you.

A Tropical Glass of Chia

Preparation time: 10 minutes

Cooking time: 0 minutes

Servings: 1

Ingredients:

   1 cup coconut water

   1 tablespoon chia seeds

   1 cup pineapple, sliced

   1/2 cup mango, sliced

Directions:

   Add all the listed **Ingredients:** to a blender

   Blend until you have a smooth and creamy
      texture

   Serve chilled and enjoy!

Nutrition:

Calories: 90

Fat: 5g

Carbohydrates: 11g

Protein: 4g

Simple Anti-Aging Cacao Dream

Preparation time: 10 minutes

Cooking time: 0 minutes

Servings: 1

Ingredients:

1 cup unsweetened almond milk

1 tablespoon cacao powder

6 strawberries

1 banana

Directions:

Add all the listed **Ingredients:** to a blender

Blend until you have a smooth and creamy

texture

Serve chilled and enjoy!

Nutrition:

Calories: 220

Fat: 9g

Carbohydrates: 20g

Protein: 6g

The Gut Heavy Smoothie

Preparation time: 10 minutes

Cooking time: 0 minutes

Servings: 1

Ingredients:

2-3 cups spinach leaves

1/2 cup frozen blueberries, unsweetened

1 serving aloe vera leaves

1/2 cup plain full-Fat yogurt

1 scoop Pinnaclife prebiotic Fiber

1 and 1/2 tablespoons coconut oil, unrefined

1 tablespoon chia seeds

1 tablespoon hemp hearts

1 cup of water

Directions:

Add listed **Ingredients:** to a blender

Blend until you have a smooth and creamy
texture

Serve chilled and enjoy!

Nutrition:

Calories: 409

Fat: 33g

Carbohydrates: 8g

Protein: 12g

Fresh Purple Fig Smoothie

Preparation time: 5 minutes

Cooking time: 0 minutes

Servings: 2

Ingredients:

    1 fig

    1 cup grapes

    1/2 teaspoon maqui powder

    1 cup of water

    1 pear, chopped

Directions:

    Add all the listed **Ingredients:** to a blender

    Blend until you have a smooth and creamy texture

    Serve chilled and enjoy!

Nutrition:

Calories: 136

Fat: 4g

Carbohydrates: 28g

Protein: 3g

Mesmerizing Strawberry and Chocolate Shake

Preparation time: 10 minutes

Cooking time: 0 minutes

Servings: 1

Ingredients:

   1/2 cup strawberry, sliced

   1 tablespoons coconut flake, unsweetened

   1 and 1/2 cups of water

   1/2 cup heavy cream, liquid

   1 tablespoon cocoa powder

   1 pack stevia

Directions:

   Add all the listed **Ingredients:** to a blender

   Blend on medium until you have a smooth

   Serve chilled and enjoy!

Nutrition:

Calories: 470

Fat: 46g

Carbohydrates: 15g

Protein: 4g

The Strawberry Almond Smoothie

Preparation time: 10 minutes

Cooking time: 0 minutes

Servings: 1

Ingredients:

   1/4 cup frozen strawberries, unsweetened

   16 ounces unsweetened almond milk, vanilla

   1 scoop vanilla whey Protein

   1 pack stevia

   4 ounces heavy cream

Directions:

   Add all the listed **Ingredients:** into your
      blender

   Blend until smooth

   Serve chilled and enjoy!

Nutrition:

Calories: 304

Fat: 25g

Carbohydrates: 7g

Protein: 15g

Hazelnut and Coconut Medley

Preparation time: 10 minutes

Cooking time: 0 minutes

Servings: 1

Ingredients:

 1/4 cup hazelnuts, chopped

 1/2 cup of coconut milk

 1 pack stevia

 1 and 1/2 cups of water

Directions:

 Add all the listed **Ingredients:** into your
 blender

 Blend until smooth

 Serve chilled and enjoy!

Nutrition:

Calories: 457

Fat: 46g

Carbohydrates: 12g

Protein: 7g

Overloaded Hazelnut and Mocha Shake

Preparation time: 10 minutes

Cooking time: 0 minutes

Servings: 1

Ingredients:

   1-ounce Hazelnuts

   2 cups brewed coffee, chilled

   1 tablespoon MCT oil

   2 tablespoons cocoa powder

   1-2 packet Stevia, optional

Directions:

   Add all the listed **Ingredients:** into your
      blender

   Blend until smooth

   Serve chilled and enjoy!

Nutrition:

Calories: 325

Fat: 33g

Carbohydrates: 12g

Protein: 6.8g

The Nutty Smoothie

Preparation time: 10 minutes

Cooking time: 0 minutes

Servings: 1

Ingredients:

 1-ounce Hazelnut

 1 ounce Macadamia Nuts

 1 tablespoon chia seeds

 1-2 packets Stevia, optional

 2 cups of water

Directions:

 Add all the listed **Ingredients:** to a blender

 Blend on high until smooth and creamy

 Enjoy your smoothie!

Nutrition:

Calories: 452

Fat: 43g

Carbohydrates: 15g

Protein: 9g

The Feisty Nut Shake

Preparation time: 10 minutes

Cooking time: 0 minutes

Servings: 1

Ingredients:

   1/4 cup almonds, sliced

   1/4 cup macadamia nuts, whole

   1 tablespoon flaxseed

   1/4 cup heavy cream, liquid

   1/2 tablespoon cocoa powder

   1 cup of water

   1 tablespoon hemp seed

   1 pack stevia

Directions:

   Add listed **Ingredients:** to a blender

   Blend until you have a smooth and creamy
      texture

   Serve chilled and enjoy!

Nutrition:

Calories: 590

Fat: 57g

Carbohydrates: 17g

Protein: 12g

Cayenne Spices Chocolate Shake

Preparation time: 10 minutes

Cooking time: 0 minutes

Servings: 1

Ingredients:

   1/2 pinch cayenne powder

   2 tablespoons coconut oil, unrefined

   1/4 cup coconut cream

   1 tablespoon chia seeds, whole

   2 tablespoons cacao

   Dash of vanilla extract

   1/2 1 cup water

   Ice cubes

Directions:

   Add listed **Ingredients:** to a blender

   Blend until you have a smooth and creamy
      texture

   Serve chilled and enjoy!

Nutrition:

Calories: 258

Fat: 26g

Carbohydrates: 3g

Protein: 3g

Apple Celery Detox Smoothie

Preparation time: 10 minutes

Cooking time: 0 minutes

Servings: 2

Ingredients:

   3 tablespoons collard greens

   2 ribs celery

   3 springs mint

   1 apple, chopped

   2 tablespoons hazelnuts, raw

   1/2 teaspoon moringa

   1 cup of water

   1 cup ice

Directions:

   Add all the listed **Ingredients:** to a blender

   Blend until you have a smooth and creamy
      texture

   Serve chilled and enjoy!

Nutrition:

Calories: 115

Fat: 5g

Carbohydrates: 14g

Protein: 3g

Zucchini Detox Smoothie

Preparation time: 10 minutes

Cooking time: 0 minutes

Servings: 1

Ingredients:

 1 zucchini

 1 tablespoon sea beans

 1/2 lemon, juiced

 1 teaspoon maqui berry powder

 8 tablespoons grape tomatoes

 6 tablespoons celery stocks

 1/2 jalapeno pepper, seeded

 1 cup of water

 1 cup ice

Directions:

 Add all the listed **Ingredients:** to blender
   except zucchini

 Add zucchini and blend the mixture

 Blend until smooth

 Serve chilled and enjoy!

Nutrition: Calories: 50, Fat: 0.5g, Carbohydrates: 10g

Protein: 2.4g

Carrot Detox Smoothie

Preparation time: 10 minutes

Cooking time: 0 minutes

Servings: 2

Ingredients:

    10 tablespoons carrot, chopped

    1-inch ginger, peeled and chopped

    1 teaspoon cinnamon

    1 banana, peeled

    1-inch turmeric peeled, chopped

    1 cup of coconut milk

    1 cup ice

Directions:

    Add all the listed **Ingredients:** to a blender

    Blend until smooth

    Serve chilled and enjoy!

Nutrition:

Calories: 134

Fat: 3g

Carbohydrates: 30g

Protein: 2g

Pear Jicama Detox Smoothie

Preparation time: 10 minutes

Cooking time: 0 minutes

Servings: 2

Ingredients:

3 tablespoons red kale

8 tablespoons jicama, peeled and chopped

1 lemon, juiced

1 pear, chopped

1 teaspoon reishi mushroom

1 tablespoon flaxseed

1 cup of water

1 cup ice

Directions:

Add all the listed **Ingredients:** to a blender

Blend until smooth

Serve chilled and enjoy!

Nutrition:

Calories: 102

Fat: 0g

Carbohydrates: 24g, Protein: 2g

Coconut Pineapple Detox Smoothie

Preparation time: 10 minutes

Cooking time: 0 minutes

Servings: 2

Ingredients:

3 tablespoons Swiss Chard

2 tablespoons coconut flakes

1 tablespoon chia seeds

8 tablespoons pineapple, peeled and chopped

1/2 avocado pitted

1 orange, peeled

1 cup of water

1 cup ice

Directions:

Add all the listed **Ingredients:** to a blender

Blend until smooth

Serve chilled and enjoy!

Nutrition:

Calories: 212

Fat: 0g, Carbohydrates: 26g, Protein: 3g

Pineapple Coconut Detox Smoothie

Preparation time: 10 minutes

Cooking time: 0 minutes

Servings: 2

Ingredients:

    4 cups kale, chopped

    2 cups of coconut water

    2 bananas

    2 cups pineapple

Directions:

    Add all the listed **Ingredients:** to a blender

    Blend until you have a smooth and creamy
        texture

    Serve chilled and enjoy!

Nutrition:

Calories: 299

Fat: 1.1g

Carbohydrates: 71.5g

Protein: 7.9g

Avocado Detox Smoothie

Preparation time: 10 minutes

Cooking time: 0 minutes

Servings: 3

Ingredients:

   4 cups spinach, chopped

   1 avocado, chopped

   3 cups apple juice

   2 apples, unpeeled, cored and chopped

Directions:

   Add all the listed **Ingredients:** to a blender

Blend until you have a smooth and creamy

texture

Serve chilled and enjoy!

Nutrition:

Calories: 336

Fat: 13.8g

Carbohydrates: 55.8g

Protein: 3g

Lemon Lime Lavender Smoothie

Preparation time: 10 minutes

Cooking time: 0 minutes

Servings: 3

Ingredients:

1½ cups of plant yogurt

3 tablespoons of lemon juice

4 tablespoons of lime juice

A drop of lavender extract, culinary or ½ teaspoon of culinary lavender buds

¼ cup of ice

½ teaspoon of turmeric (or even more to accomplish the desired color)

¼ cup of shavings from fresh organic lemons and limes

Directions:

Combine all of the ingredients in a blender and serve chilled with citrus shavings and lavender buds at the top for a robust scent while you spoon!

Then add plant-based milk to a thin mixture.

Nutrition:
Calories: 229

Fat: 1.1g

Carbohydrates: 71.5g

Protein: 7.9g

Jalapeno Lime and Mango Protein Smoothie

Preparation time: 10 minutes

Cooking time: 0 minutes

Servings: 2

Ingredients:

A little banana

1 Cheribundi Tart Cherry Mango smoothie pack (or ¾ cup frozen mango)

A heaping tablespoon of chopped jalapeño (about ½ a little pepper)

1 cup unsweetened original almond milk (or coconut milk)

1 tablespoon flaxseed, ground

1 tablespoon chia seeds, ground

2 tablespoons hemp seed, ground

½ lime, newly squeezed

½ an avocado (optional)

Directions:

Combine all of the ingredients within a blender and work for approximately 45 seconds until smooth.

Pour right into a glass and revel in!

Nutrition:

Calories: 219

Fat: 1.1g

Carbohydrates: 1.5g

Protein: 7.9g

Cinnamon Apple Smoothie

Preparation time: 10 minutes

Cooking time: 0 minutes

Servings: 2

Ingredients:

   1 small apple, sliced

   ½ cup of rolled oats

   ½ teaspoon of cinnamon

   ½ teaspoon of nutmeg

   1 tablespoon almond butter

   ½ cup of unsweetened coconut milk three to
      four ice

   ½ cup of cool water

Directions:

Combine oats and water inside a blender and
   allow it to rest for two minutes; therefore,
   the oats can soften.

Bring all of the remaining ingredients to the
   blender and blend for approximately 30
   seconds until smooth.

Pour right into a glass and sprinkle with just a little spare cinnamon and nutmeg. Enjoy!

Nutrition:

Calories: 232

Fat: 1.1g

Carbohydrates: 14.5g

Protein: 7.9g

Drinks

Banana Weight Loss Juice

Preparation Time: 10 Minutes

Cooking Time: 0 Minutes

Servings: 1

Ingredients:

- Water (1/3 C.)
- Apple (1, Sliced)
- Orange (1, Sliced)
- Banana (1, Sliced)
- Lemon Juice (1 T.)

Directions:

1. Looking to boost your weight loss? The key is taking in less Calories; this recipe can get you there.
2. Simply place everything into your blender, blend on high for twenty seconds, and then pour into your glass.

Nutrition:

Calories: 289

Total Carbohydrate: 2 g

Cholesterol: 3 mg

Total Fat: 17 g

Fiber: 2 g

Protein: 7 g

Sodium: 163 mg

Citrus Detox Juice

Preparation Time: 10 Minutes

Cooking Time: 0 Minutes

Servings: 4

Ingredients:

- Water (3 C.)
- Lemon (1, Sliced)
- Grapefruit (1, Sliced)
- Orange (1, Sliced)

Directions:

1. While starting your new diet, it is going to be vital to stay hydrated. This detox juice is the perfect solution and offers some extra flavor.
2. Begin by peeling and slicing up your fruit. Once this is done, place in a pitcher of water and infuse the water overnight.

Nutrition:

Calories: 269

Total Carbohydrate: 2 g

Cholesterol: 3 mg

Total Fat: 14 g

Fiber: 2 g

Protein: 7 g

Sodium: 183 mg

Metabolism Water

Preparation Time: 10 Minutes

Cooking Time: 0 Minutes

Servings: 1

Ingredients:

Water (3 C.)

Cucumber (1, Sliced)

Lemon (1, Sliced)

Mint (2 Leaves)

Ice

Directions:

At some point, we probably all wish for a quicker metabolism! With the lemon acting as an energizer, cucumber for a refreshing taste, and mint to help your stomach digest, this water is perfect!

All you will have to do is get out a pitcher, place all of the ingredients in, and allow the ingredients to soak overnight for maximum benefits!

Nutrition:

Calories: 301

Total Carbohydrate: 2 g

Cholesterol: 13 mg

Total Fat: 17 g

Fiber: 4 g

Protein: 8 g

Sodium: 201 mg

Stress Relief Detox Drink

Preparation Time: 5 Minutes

Cooking Time: 0 Minutes

Servings: 1

Ingredients:

Water (1 Pitcher)

Mint

Lemon (1, Sliced)

Basil

Strawberries (1 C., Sliced)

Ice

Directions:

Life can be a pretty stressful event. Luckily, there is water to help keep you cool, calm, and collected! The lemon works like an energizer, the basil is a natural antidepressant, and mint can help your stomach do its job better. As for the strawberries, those are just for some sweetness!

When you are ready, take all of the ingredients and place into a pitcher of water overnight and enjoy the next day.

Nutrition:

Calories: 189

Total Carbohydrate: 2 g

Cholesterol: 73 mg

Total Fat: 17 g

Fiber: 0 g

Protein: 7 g

Sodium: 163 mg

Strawberry Pink Drink

Preparation Time: 10 Minutes

Cooking Time: 5 Minutes

Servings: 4

Ingredients:

Water (1 C., Boiling)

Sugar (2 T.)

Acai Tea Bag (1)

Coconut Milk (1 C.)

Frozen Strawberries (1/2 C.)

Directions:

If you are looking for a little treat, this is going to be the recipe for you! You will begin by boiling your cup of water and seep the tea bag in for at least five minutes.

When the tea is set, add in the sugar and coconut milk. Be sure to stir well to spread the sweetness throughout the tea.

Finally, add in your strawberries, and you can enjoy your freshly made pink drink!

Nutrition:

Calories: 321

Total Carbohydrate: 2 g

Cholesterol: 13 mg

Total Fat: 17 g

Fiber: 2 g

Protein: 9 g

Sodium: 312 mg

Avocado Pudding

Preparation Time: 10 minutes

Cooking Time: 0 minute

Servings: 8

Ingredients:

2 ripe avocados, peeled, pitted and cut into pieces

1 tbsp fresh lime juice

14 oz can coconut milk

80 drops of liquid stevia

2 tsp vanilla extract

Directions:

Add all ingredients into the blender and blend until smooth.

Serve and enjoy.

Nutrition:

Calories: 209

Total Carbohydrate: 6 g

Cholesterol: 13 mg

Total Fat: 7 g

Fiber: 2 g

Protein: 17 g , Sodium: 193 mg

Almond Butter Brownies

Preparation Time: 10 minutes

Cooking Time: 20 minutes

Servings: 4

Ingredients:

1 scoop Protein powder

2 tbsp cocoa powder

1/2 cup almond butter, melted

1 cup bananas, overripe

Directions:

Preheat the oven to 350 F/ 176 C.

Spray brownie tray with cooking spray.

Add all ingredients into the blender and blend until
smooth.

Pour batter into the prepared dish and bake in
preheated oven for 20 minutes.

Serve and enjoy.

Nutrition:

Calories: 214

Total Carbohydrate: 2 g

Cholesterol: 73 mg

Total Fat: 7 g

Fiber: 2g

Protein: 19 g

Sodium: 308 g

Raspberry Chia Pudding

Preparation Time: 3 hours 10 minutes

Cooking Time: 0 minute

Servings: 2

Ingredients:

   4 tbsp chia seeds

   1 cup coconut milk

   1/2 cup raspberries

Directions:

   Add raspberry and coconut milk in a blender and
      blend until smooth.

Pour mixture into the Mason jar.

Add chia seeds in a jar and stir well.

Close jar tightly with lid and shake well.

Place in refrigerator for 3 hours.

Serve chilled and enjoy.

Nutrition:

Calories: 189

Total Carbohydrate: 6 g

Cholesterol: 3 mg

Total Fat: 7 g

Fiber: 4 g

Protein: 12 g

Sodium: 293 mg

Chocolate Fudge

Preparation Time: 10 minutes

Cooking Time: 0 minute

Servings: 12

Ingredients:

   4 oz unsweetened dark chocolate

   3/4 cup coconut butter

   15 drops liquid stevia

   1 tsp vanilla extract

Directions:

Melt coconut butter and dark chocolate.

Add ingredients to the large bowl and combine well.

Pour mixture into a silicone loaf pan and place in
   refrigerator until set.

Cut into pieces and serve.

Nutrition:

Calories: 283

Total Carbohydrate: 10 g

Cholesterol: 3 mg

Total Fat: 8 g

Fiber: 2 g

Protein: 9 g

Sodium: 271 mg

Quick Chocó Brownie

Preparation Time: 10 minutes

Cooking Time: 2 minutes

Servings: 1

Ingredients:

- 1/4 cup almond milk
- 1 tbsp cocoa powder
- 1 scoop chocolate Protein powder
- 1/2 tsp baking powder

Directions:

In a microwave-safe mug blend together baking powder, Protein powder, and cocoa.

Add almond milk in a mug and stir well.

Place mug in microwave and microwave for 30 seconds.

Serve and enjoy.

Nutrition:

Calories: 231

Total Carbohydrate: 2 g

Cholesterol: 13 mg

Total Fat: 15 g

Fiber: 2 g

Protein: 8 g

Sodium: 298 mg

Simple Almond Butter Fudge

Preparation Time: 15 minutes

Cooking Time: 0 minutes

Servings: 8

Ingredients:

　　1/2 cup almond butter

　　15 drops liquid stevia

　　2 1/2 tbsp coconut oil

Directions:

Combine together almond butter and coconut oil in a saucepan. Gently warm until melted.

Add stevia and stir well.

Pour mixture into the candy container and place in refrigerator until set.

Serve and enjoy.

Nutrition:

Calories: 198

Total Carbohydrate: 5 g

Cholesterol: 12 mg

Total Fat: 10 g

Fiber: 2 g

Protein: 6 g

Sodium: 257 mg

Coconut Peanut Butter Fudge

Preparation Time: 1 hour 15 minutes

Cooking Time: 0 minute

Servings: 20

Ingredients:

12 oz smooth peanut butter

3 tbsp coconut oil

4 tbsp coconut cream

15 drops liquid stevia

Pinch of salt

Directions:

Line baking tray with parchment paper.

Melt coconut oil in a saucepan over low heat.

Add peanut butter, coconut cream, stevia, and salt in a saucepan. Stir well.

Pour fudge mixture into the prepared baking tray and place in refrigerator for 1 hour.

Cut into pieces and serve.

Nutrition:

Calories: 189

Total Carbohydrate: 2 g

Cholesterol: 13 mg

Total Fat: 7 g

Fiber: 2 g

Protein: 10 g

Sodium: 301 mg

Lemon Mousse

Preparation Time: 10 minutes

Cooking Time: 0 minute

Servings: 2

Ingredients:

 14 oz coconut milk

 12 drops liquid stevia

 1/2 tsp lemon extract

 1/4 tsp turmeric

Directions:

Place coconut milk can in the refrigerator for
 overnight. Scoop out thick cream into a mixing
 bowl.

Add remaining ingredients to the bowl and whip
 using a hand mixer until smooth.

Transfer mousse mixture to a zip-lock bag and pipe
 into small serving glasses. Place in refrigerator.

Serve chilled and enjoy.

Nutrition:

Calories: 189

Total Carbohydrate: 2 g

Cholesterol: 13 mg

Total Fat: 7 g

Fiber: 2 g

Protein: 15 g

 Sodium: 321 mg

Chocó Chia Pudding

Preparation Time: 10 minutes

Cooking Time: 0 minutes

Servings: 6

Ingredients:

  2 1/2 cups coconut milk

2 scoops stevia extract powder

6 tbsp cocoa powder

1/2 cup chia seeds

1/2 tsp vanilla extract

1/8 cup xylitol

1/8 tsp salt

Directions:

Add all ingredients into the blender and blend until
  smooth.

Pour mixture into the glass container and place in
  refrigerator.

Serve chilled and enjoy.

Nutrition:

Calories: 178

Total Carbohydrate: 3 g

Cholesterol: 3 mg

Total Fat: 17 g

Fiber: g

Protein: 9 g

Sodium: 297 mg

Spiced Buttermilk

Preparation Time: 5 minutes

Cooking Time: 0 minute

Servings: 2

Ingredients:

3/4 teaspoon ground cumin

1/4 teaspoon sea salt

1/8 teaspoon ground black pepper

2 mint leaves

1/8 teaspoon lemon juice

¼ cup cilantro leaves

1 cup of chilled water

1 cup vegan yogurt, unsweetened

Ice as needed

Directions:

Place all the ingredients in the order in a food processor or blender, except for cilantro and ¼ teaspoon cumin, and then pulse for 2 to 3 minutes at high speed until smooth.

Pour the milk into glasses, top with cilantro and cumin, and then serve.

Nutrition:

Calories: 211

Total Carbohydrate: 7 g

Cholesterol: 13 mg

Total Fat: 18 g

Fiber: 3 g

Protein: 17 g

Sodium: 289 mg

Turmeric Lassi

Preparation Time: 5 minutes

Cooking Time: 0 minute

Servings: 2

Ingredients:

- 1 teaspoon grated ginger
- 1/8 teaspoon ground black pepper
- 1 teaspoon turmeric powder
- 1/8 teaspoon cayenne
- 1 tablespoon coconut sugar
- 1/8 teaspoon salt
- 1 cup vegan yogurt
- 1 cup almond milk

Directions:

1. Place all the ingredients in the order in a food processor or blender and then pulse for 2 to 3 minutes at high speed until smooth.
2. Pour the lassi into two glasses and then serve.

Nutrition:

Calories: 392

Fat: 10g

Protein: 18g

Sugar: 8g

Brownie Batter Orange Chia Shake

Preparation Time: 5 minutes

Cooking Time: 0 minute

Servings: 2

Ingredients:

  2 tablespoons cocoa powder

  3 tablespoons chia seeds

  ¼ teaspoon salt

  4 tablespoons chocolate chips

  4 teaspoons coconut sugar

  ½ teaspoon orange zest

  ½ teaspoon vanilla extract, unsweetened

  2 cup almond milk

Directions:

Place all the ingredients in the order in a food processor or blender and then pulse for 2 to 3 minutes at high speed until smooth.

Pour the smoothie into two glasses and then serve.

Nutrition:

Calories: 290

Fat: 11g

Protein: 20g

Sugar: 9g

Saffron Pistachio Beverage

Preparation Time: 5 minutes

Cooking Time: 0 minute

Servings: 2

Ingredients:

   8 strands of saffron

   1 tablespoon cashews

   1/4 teaspoon ground ginger

   2 tablespoons pistachio

   1/8 teaspoon cloves

   1/4 teaspoon ground black pepper

   1/4 teaspoon cardamom powder

   3 tablespoons coconut sugar

   1/4 teaspoon cinnamon

   1/8 teaspoon fennel seeds

   1/4 teaspoon poppy seeds

Directions:

Place all the ingredients in the order in a food
   processor or blender and then pulse for 2 to 3
   minutes at high speed until smooth.

Pour the smoothie into two glasses and then serve.

Nutrition:

Calories: 394, Fat: 5g, Protein: 12g, Sugar: 4g

Mexican Hot Chocolate Mix

Preparation Time: 5 minutes

Cooking Time: 0 minute

Servings: 2

Ingredients:

For the Hot Chocolate Mix:

- 1/3 cup chopped dark chocolate
- 1/8 teaspoon cayenne
- 1/8 teaspoon salt
- 1/2 teaspoon cinnamon
- 1/4 cup coconut sugar
- 1 teaspoon cornstarch
- 3 tablespoons cocoa powder
- 1/2 teaspoon vanilla extract, unsweetened

Directions:

Place all the ingredients of hot chocolate mix in the order in a food processor or blender and then pulse for 2 to 3 minutes at high speed until ground.

Nutrition:

Calories: 160

Fat: 6g

Protein: 26g, Sugar: 7g

Pumpkin Spice Frappuccino

Preparation Time: 5 minutes

Cooking Time: 0 minute

Servings: 2

Ingredients:

½ teaspoon ground ginger

1/8 teaspoon allspice

½ teaspoon ground cinnamon

2 tablespoons coconut sugar

1/8 teaspoon nutmeg

¼ teaspoon ground cloves

1 teaspoon vanilla extract, unsweetened

2 teaspoons instant coffee

2 cups almond milk, unsweetened

1 cup of ice cubes

Directions:

Place all the ingredients in the order in a food processor or blender and then pulse for 2 to 3 minutes at high speed until smooth.

Pour the Frappuccino into two glasses and then serve.

Nutrition:

Calories: 490

Fat: 9g, Protein: 12g, Sugar: 11g

Cookie Dough Milkshake

Preparation Time: 5 minutes

Cooking Time: 0 minute

Servings: 2

Ingredients:

2 tablespoons cookie dough

5 dates, pitted

2 teaspoons chocolate chips

1/2 teaspoon vanilla extract, unsweetened

1/2 cup almond milk, unsweetened

1 ½ cup almond milk ice cubes

Directions:

Place all the ingredients in the order in a food processor or blender and then pulse for 2 to 3 minutes at high speed until smooth.

Pour the milkshake into two glasses and then serve with some cookie dough balls.

Nutrition:

Calories: 240

Fat: 13g

Protein: 21g, Sugar: 9g

Strawberry and Hemp Smoothie

Preparation Time: 5 minutes

Cooking Time: 0 minute

Servings: 2

Ingredients:

3 cups fresh strawberries

2 tablespoons hemp seeds

1/2 teaspoon vanilla extract, unsweetened

1/8 teaspoon sea salt

2 tablespoons maple syrup

1 cup vegan yogurt

1 cup almond milk, unsweetened

1 cup of ice cubes

2 tablespoons hemp Protein

Directions:

Place all the ingredients in the order in a food processor or blender, except for Protein powder, and then pulse for 2 to 3 minutes at high speed until smooth.

Pour the smoothie into two glasses and then serve.

Nutrition:

Calories: 510

Fat: 18g

Protein: 26g, Sugar: 12g

Blueberry, Hazelnut and Hemp Smoothie

Preparation Time: 5 minutes

Cooking Time: 0 minute

Servings: 2

Ingredients:

2 tablespoons hemp seeds

1 ½ cups frozen blueberries

2 tablespoons chocolate Protein powder

1/2 teaspoon vanilla extract, unsweetened

2 tablespoons chocolate hazelnut butter

1 small frozen banana

3/4 cup almond milk

Directions:

Place all the ingredients in the order in a food processor or blender and then pulse for 2 to 3 minutes at high speed until smooth.

Pour the smoothie into two glasses and then serve.

Nutrition:

Calories: 195

Fat: 14g, Protein: 36g, Sugar: 10g

Mango Lassi

Preparation Time: 5 minutes

Cooking Time: 0 minute

Servings: 2

Ingredients:

 1 ¼ cup mango pulp

 1 tablespoon coconut sugar

 1/8 teaspoon salt

 1/2 teaspoon lemon juice

 1/4 cup almond milk, unsweetened

 1/4 cup chilled water

 1 cup cashew yogurt

Directions:

Place all the ingredients in the order in a food processor or blender and then pulse for 2 to 3 minutes at high speed until smooth.

Pour the lassi into two glasses and then serve.

Nutrition:

Calories: 420

Fat: 12g

Protein: 23g

Sugar: 13g

Mocha Chocolate Shake

Preparation Time: 5 minutes

Cooking Time: 0 minute

Servings: 2

Ingredients:

1/4 cup hemp seeds

2 teaspoons cocoa powder, unsweetened

1/2 cup dates, pitted

1 tablespoon instant coffee powder

2 tablespoons flax seeds

2 1/2 cups almond milk, unsweetened

1/2 cup crushed ice

Directions:

Place all the ingredients in the order in a food processor or blender and then pulse for 2 to 3 minutes at high speed until smooth.

Pour the smoothie into two glasses and then serve.

Nutrition:

Calories: 432

Fat: 18g

Protein: 14g, Sugar: 12g

Chard, Lettuce and Ginger Smoothie

Preparation Time: 5 minutes

Cooking Time: 0 minute

Servings: 2

Ingredients:

10 Chard leaves, chopped

1-inch piece of ginger, chopped

10 lettuce leaves, chopped

½ teaspoon black salt

2 pear, chopped

2 teaspoons coconut sugar

¼ teaspoon ground black pepper

¼ teaspoon salt

2 tablespoons lemon juice

2 cups of water

Directions:

Place all the ingredients in the order in a food processor or blender and then pulse for 2 to 3 minutes at high speed until smooth.

Pour the smoothie into two glasses and then serve.

Nutrition:

Calories: 240

Fat: 4g, Protein: 16g, Sugar: 3g

Red Beet, Pear and Apple Smoothie

Preparation Time: 5 minutes

Cooking Time: 0 minute

Servings: 2

Ingredients:

- 1/2 of medium beet, peeled, chopped
- 1 tablespoon chopped cilantro
- 1 orange, juiced
- 1 medium pear, chopped
- 1 medium apple, cored, chopped
- 1/4 teaspoon ground black pepper
- 1/8 teaspoon rock salt
- 1 teaspoon coconut sugar
- 1/4 teaspoons salt
- 1 cup of water

Directions:

Place all the ingredients in the order in a food processor or blender and then pulse for 2 to 3 minutes at high speed until smooth.

Pour the smoothie into two glasses and then serve.

Nutrition:

Calories: 240

Fat: 4g, Protein: 16g, Sugar: 3g

Berry and Yogurt Smoothie

Preparation Time: 5 minutes

Cooking Time: 0 minute

Servings: 2

Ingredients:

   2 small bananas

   3 cups frozen mixed berries

   1 ½ cup cashew yogurt

   1/2 teaspoon vanilla extract, unsweetened

   1/2 cup almond milk, unsweetened

Directions:

   Place all the ingredients in the order in a food
      processor or blender and then pulse for 2 to 3
      minutes at high speed until smooth.

   Pour the smoothie into two glasses and then serve.

Nutrition:

Calories: 291

Fat: 9g

Protein: 17g

Sugar: 5g

Chocolate and Cherry Smoothie

Preparation Time: 5 minutes

Cooking Time: 0 minute

Servings: 2

Ingredients:

4 cups frozen cherries

2 tablespoons cocoa powder

1 scoop of Protein powder

1 teaspoon maple syrup

2 cups almond milk, unsweetened

Directions:

Place all the ingredients in the order in a food processor or blender and then pulse for 2 to 3 minutes at high speed until smooth.

Pour the smoothie into two glasses and then serve.

Nutrition:

Calories: 247

Fat: 3g

Protein: 18g

Sugar: 3g

Conclusion

In a nutshell, this cookbook offers you a world full of options to diversify your plant-based menu. People on this diet are usually seen struggling to choose between healthy food and flavor but, soon, they run out of the options. The selection of 250 recipes in this book is enough to adorn your dinner table with flavorsome, plant-based meals every day. Give each recipe a good read and try them out in the kitchen. You will experience tempting aromas and binding flavors every day.

The book is conceptualized with the idea of offering you a comprehensive view of a plant-based diet and how it can benefit the body. You may find the shift sudden, especially if you are a die-hard fan of non-vegetarian items. But you need not give up anything that you love. Eat everything in moderation.

The next step is to start experimenting with the different recipes in this book and see which ones are your favorites. Everyone has their favorite food, and you will surely find several of yours in this book. Start with breakfast and work your way through. You will be pleasantly surprised at how tasty a vegan meal really can be.

You will love reading this book, as it helps you to understand how revolutionary a plant-based diet can be. It will help you to make informed decisions as you move toward greater change for the greater good. What are you waiting for? Have you begun your journey on the path of the plant-based diet yet? If you haven't, do it now! Now you have everything you need to get started making budget-friendly, healthy plant-based recipes. Just follow your basic shopping list and follow your meal plan to get started! It's easy to switch over to a plant-based diet if you have your meals planned out and temptation locked away. Don't forget to clean out your kitchen before starting, and you're sure to meet all your diet and health goals.

You need to plan if you are thinking about dieting. First, you can start slowly by just eating one meal a day, which is vegetarian and gradually increasing your number of vegetarian meals. Whenever you are struggling, ask your friend or family member to support you and keep you motivated. One important thing is also to be regularly accountable for not following the diet.

If dieting seems very important to you and you need to do it right, then it is recommended that you visit a professional such as a nutritionist or dietitian to discuss your dieting plan and optimizing it for the better.

No matter how much you want to lose weight, it is not advised that you decrease your calorie intake to an unhealthy level. Losing weight does not mean that you stop eating. It is done by carefully planning meals.

A plant-based diet is very easy once you get into it. At first, you will start to face a lot of difficulties, but if you start slowly, then you can face all the barriers and achieve your goal.

Swap out one unhealthy food item each week that you know is not helping you and put in its place one of the plant-based ingredients that you like. Then have some fun creating the many different recipes in this book. Find out what recipes you like the most so you can make them often and most of all; have some fun exploring all your recipe options.

Wish you good luck with the plant-based diet!

CPSIA information can be obtained
at www.ICGtesting.com
Printed in the USA
BVHW052031120421
604748BV00001B/52

9 781801 833387